Serenade

Serenade

poems by

Isabel Bermudez

with illustrations by

Simon Turvey

Paekakariki Press

2020

This is number 5
of an edition of 250 copies

ISBN 9781908133403

Typeset in 12pt 'Monotype' Garamond 156
Printed and published by Paekakariki Press,
Walthamstow

Acknowledgements

'Serenade' *The Winchester Poetry Prize Winners Anthology 2018;* 'Dulces de Isabel la Católica', 'Master of Works' *The New European Newspaper;* 'Postcolonial' appeared in the anthology *Spring of the Muses* ed. Deborah Gaye, (Avalanche Books, Bristol, 2019).

Contents

Río Claro

Polished lime-stone, smooth edges
pale beneath the clear water,
luminous as newly-laid eggs, the river's fruit.

Sun-spots dance, one fish and then another,
a play of sun that leads a life of its own,
bottom-dweller, at one remove.

Here in the mountains, warring factions
raid sleep's borderlands
and the river carves her long and complicated history:

los paras with their rhetoric of purity,
la guerrilla—marching leaf-cutter ants,
and innocence—this brilliant white light—

the river wears it like a new dress
slips it over a layer of bones.

Duende

I lift my arms,
then let them drop,
try to right myself, stand straight,
the shadow moves with me.
Arms, locked to their joints,
I raise my right arm, the shadow too,
raises his. And my left leg.
And my hand. The briefest of delays
as the machine reads my skeleton.
I click my fingers. Who'd resist
the snap of those castanets?
A small time lapse.
The joints and shadows roll.
It is, I have to say, grotesque.

Arms oustretched at right-angles,
legs planted firm and wide
the perfect specimen of Vitruvian Man
is painted on the screen before me.
Superimposed upon him,
my shaky armature lists to one side.
Life slowly eats away,
my neck's adorned now with her spurs,
the wear and tear of curving, pterodactyl bone.

And this dark ancestral bird
in Sunday black,
all talon and huge wings,
inhabits his cage of flesh:
my crooked, diffident shadow,
I pull your strings,
feed you with my soul.

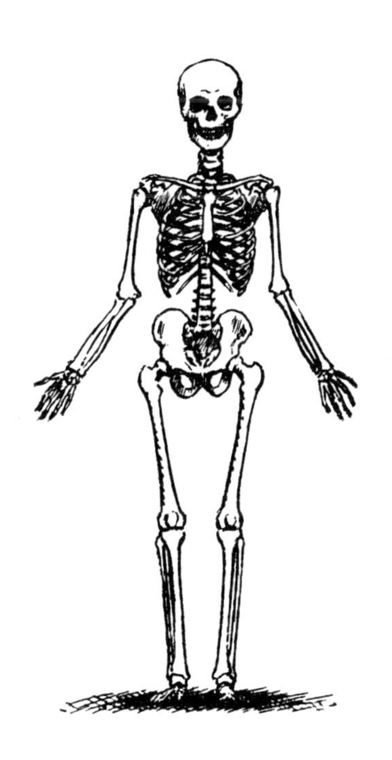

Quinces

Bulbous, the quinces sit
on a turquoise platter.

Skin puckers:
roughness, dimple, nick, scar.

Poised, they balance,
a rich expanse of flesh,

heavy chess pieces,
freighted years.

Each, a late Rembrandt—
brush in hand, puffy-faced—

after life has done with them
what it does with us all:

every disguise gone,
left to evening light,

a night candle
and late, clear birdsong

which lives, like the worm
in their yellow orb.

Gazpacho

A kickback of chilli.
Ice cubes rattle in the pot.

I clink my spoon: sound
of bells or horses' hooves,

a beggar rattling his tin.
Gazpacho thrills,

soothes, chills: water at
the splitting point

as it tips over rock.
A scalded hand

under the cold tap
Sailors on the *Santa María*,

eating dry bread, garlic, oil:
kick of a mule

on the wretched
slopes of the Andes;

tomatoes and peppers,
those things

seeded in the Old World
O child of the New—

green, bitter, true.

Postcolonial

There is a certain kind of Englishman
who will adopt your country.
He'll know it better than you do.
He'll even speak the language, if imperfectly.
He'll go to parties with all the 'in' people.
Soon, he'll be advising ministers on
Peace, War and Poverty,
before sailing down the Río Magdalena
escorted by the FARC.
He'll visit cocaine labs and the best hotels.
First and foremost, he's an amateur, an enthusiast,
bred on the playing fields of Wellington and Winchester.
He'll return with his loot of film and tales,
dine out on them for years. But there's one thing
that has him flummoxed (and I've a soft spot
for this Englishman). For the life of him, he can't dance.

Venus and Mars

Two Sèvres porcelain vases
covered in gold leaf,
nude nymphs
cascading down the sides.

Shipped in the nineteenth century
from Paris to Cartagena,
a gift such as Louis XV
gave to Mme de Pompadour;
they travelled by mule
over the cordillera
from Honda in Tolima, to Bogotá.

They bobbed hundreds of miles,
mouths open,
lurching over the mountains.
And not a crack, not a chip,
just here and there,
the loss of some leaf.
Each individually signed.

For the white and pink and blue
empty amphoras tossed about
on the new continent,
for water unpoured, poured.
For heat and mosquitos,
mud and freezing nights
around a brazier.

For a patina of mist
burnt off after dawn,
for the watchmen on love's journey
and the sheer lunacy of it all,
I have instead
these lines,
amor.

Ávila

In the *estanco* they sell cigarettes,
stamps, and toys so out of date the stock piles high:
exercise books, blank squares not written in,
biros whose ink has dried up.
A miniature of the Generalissimo sits in sun in the
window,
along with tanks, flags and soldiers.
She shuffles paper in the back, he still owns the shop
which smells of Sundays.

My postcards of the Cathedral from the 1970's
will have the date and this place
stamped on them, as if to prove to the dead—
those shadows at café tables
ordering pears poached in red wine,
that I made my pilgrimage and saw them here
on our trip to Spain, in 1971.

An atmosphere so perfectly pickled
in this fortress town,
that, having escaped down to the Duero,
I am left wondering at the nightingale
whose notes are now spilling
like a bolt of cloth unwinding:
its clear song, something so precise and hard,
like a cut-glass bowl the sun strikes
and shines through.

Barrio de las Letras

A scything swoop
over the rooftops.
High on the fourth floor
a woman in her eightieth year
waters geraniums
on her narrow balcony.

She looks up, hearing
screams rain down
on Cervantes' stone
and on the convent
where a Romani gypsy
in a doorway
rolls her dead eyes upwards.
What is it, this burst of joy,
if not the returning swifts?

Echoes in city belfries,
the rattle of coins in a tin,
summoning the *enanos*
who call out to each-
other in a band of three:

Velázquez's dwarves,
guitars straddled on their backs,
faces brown as earth,
slipping out of the metro,
down blind alleys
into the Calle de Lope de Vega:
two ages colliding—
O Columbus—
shrinking like smoke
in white light and spring.

They loaded the ships

with planks, spars, bolts, nails,
potch, tar, whale oil, fat, deadeyes,
tools for carpentry, ropes and buoys;
sailcloth, leather, yarn, wax
ropes, tackle, blocks, falconets,
anchors, drags and chains;

lombards, muskets,
powder and stone balls,
scrap metal, wadding, matches;
crossbows, arrows,
helmets, shields, swords and lances;

ship's biscuits, beans, peas
wine, vinegar and medicines,
honey, syrup, water,
dried fish, salt meat, salt pork,
pigs and hens for slaughter,
salt flour, rice, cheese and almonds;

copper cauldrons,
three-legged cooking pots,
knives, ladles, measuring vessels,
bowls, candles, lamps, oil, wicks and snuffers;

steel, flint, tinder, lanterns,
firewood, manacles and leg irons;
boathooks, sweeps, buckets, mats and baskets,
fish hooks, lines, sinkers, nautical almanacs;

notebooks, account books,
tables and journals,
quills, ink, sealing wax;
charts, paper, parchment,
compasses, compass needles, magnets,
half hour glasses;

astrolabes and quadrants,
dividers and rulers,
plumbs, plumb lines, tallow;
drums, tambourines,
glass beads, gold, silver and spices—
in small quantities, as samples—

flags, bibles and penance.

Master of Works

Poem composed from an original bill, held in the Portuguese National Archive of Torre do Tombo, which a Master of Works (mestre de obras) presented in 1853 for repairs which were made to the Capela do Bom Jesus de Braga.

For correcting the ten commandments, embellishing
Our Lord and changing the cords around his tunic;
for 1 new cockerel for St Peter and for painting his crest;
for gold paint and new feathers on the Guardian Angel's
   right wing
and for washing the son of Our Lord and painting him;
for removing all stains from Tobias's son
and giving earrings to Abraham's invisible daughter;
for brightening up the flames of hell;
a Devil's tail and various adjustments to the sinners;
for a new infant to hang at the neck of Our Lady
and for all the work to the sky—

for decorating it with stars and washing the moon—
for composing Herod's hair and costume;
for retouching Purgatory and putting in new souls;
a stone at the base of David, as well as thickening Saul's
   hair (and lengthening Tobias's feet);
for decorating Noah's Ark, modelling the belly of the
   Prodigal Son and cleaning San Tinoco's left ear;
for nailing a star which had fallen from the foot of
   the Heavenly Choir;
for giving St Michael new boots and cleaning his sword
and, last but not least, for cleaning the devil's fingernails
and horns, the sum total of 2545 reales.

Old Madrid

On the stalls
by the Plaza Mayor,
bright red flamenco dresses
flame in August sun.

Each synthetic frill,
black and red,
wants for a hand
to reach out and touch it.

The man who makes music
by rubbing the rims
of two dozen wine-glasses
filled with water,
has a cardboard sign saying
Please give. I'm saving up for a Ferrari.

Old Madrid—
men on stilts
or blowing bubbles;
in a window,
the makers of religious articles
advertise *Liquidación total.*

Like elderly relatives
asleep in their chair,
the family businesses,
mantilla and cloth shops
and dusty boutiques
for ladies of a certain age,
hat-makers and Guerra Fotografía
grow dust on their sills.

We step into a cool hallway
to reach the *pensión*
on the fourth floor:
a smell of stone,
of dinner-time and meals on trays.
And, half-way up,
an open casement window
showing sheer blue
shines its light
on the musty dark
as a student in a doorway
rattles her bunch of keys,
calls time.

Columbus's Bell

Yo tengo para tí mi buen amigo un corazón de mango del Sinú
oloroso genuino amable y tierno.
I have for you, my good friend, a heart of mango from El Sinú,
pungent, kind, tender and true.

RAUL GOMEZ JATTIN

Bronze bell of the Santa María,
salvaged from the wreck of a galleon
among smatterings of gold.

Fractured, tarnished,
claimed by Portugal, retrieved by Spain,
sold at auction for millions.

Bell that roamed the oceans
startling eerily in a storm
like the cry of a lost goat.

Treasure, boasting history's green-grey patina,
the poems of Rual Gómez Jattín
are hauled to the surface again

by curious students in American universities,
thirty years on.
Madman, drunkard, seer,

scandalising the staid literary world.
Smoking marijuana in his hammock
under elegant balconies in Cartagena,

drinking deep of his *aguardiente* spring:
dreaming his boat set sail for paradise,
beside a half-moon bay of white sand:

one in a long line of the broken
whose lines ring out again in a sudden swell.
He died like a stray dog under the wheels

of a moving bus, the ghost of Columbus's bell.

Cloister

They come and go, the linnets and the sparrows,
swoop through a fine mesh protecting orange trees below.
Monks sing softly on CD from loudspeakers
and the little birds flit from gargoyle to gargoyle
telling of dusty public gardens,
of the wide Tagus with its many bridges,
spreading word of the drought down south,
of rich pickings in fennel, mallow and oat-grass
  in the fields by the river;
of sheltered courtyards with potted ferns,
  of tourists' leavings.
All this sleeping on the tongues of the *ancianos*
who have seen so many summers come and go,
who sit on park benches and round café tables—
their talk peppered with *De veras? Pero claro!*
  No fue siempre así?
Really? But of course! and Wasn't it always like this?

Dulces de Isabel la Católica

Feathery yolks
of *Yemas de Ávila,*
miniature suns
in white paper ruffs:

all the trays of *pastelería*
whose flour is weighed
in the ghostly balance
of the Puerta del Peso de la Harina.

Food of the ancestors,
adventurers and second sons
who drew the parchment maps,
plotted a course by the stars,

were incredibly brave
and incredibly cruel;
this white light cut with lemon
rising in clouds:

almonds and water and flour and oil
stuffed to the gills with sugar—
the bitter bitter bitter
dulces de Isabel la Católica.

Serenade

When the men come with hats and guitars
Welcome them, exclaim, '*Ay, los serenateros*!'
  Clasp your hands!
Do as your mother does! It's all you've ever wanted.
To be serenaded on a steaming Cartagena night.
When they come round in white trousers and shirts,
thrumming their guitars, don't shrink behind your chair.
Play your part! For God's sake, get into the spirit
  of the thing
as they break into the first vallenato, and their hard eyes
turn soft. So yes! Think of them counting the takings
in the abandoned lot. The cramped hut. The husband
  who beats his wife.
The night air's thick with rum. In the Viceroy's Palace,
here, where the ancestors disembarked,
you're a *rica,* being taken for a ride. So get on the old mule!
Hitch your skirt! And don't forget your gun!